W9-CLL-329

The Beaver: How He Works

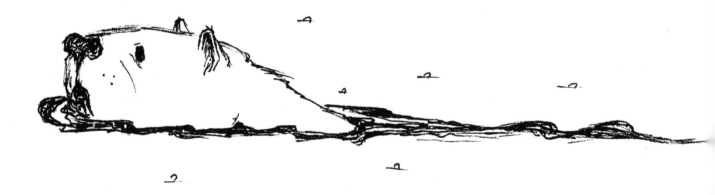

The Beaver

HOW HE WORKS

written and illustrated by Glen Rounds

Holiday House · New York

Library of Congress Cataloging in Publication Data

Rounds, Glen, 1906-
    The beaver, how he works.

    SUMMARY: Describes the life of a beaver and the
methods he uses to dam streams and build himself
a lodge.
    1. Beavers—Juvenile literature. [1. Beavers]
I. Title.
QL737.R632R68   599′.3232   76-15027
ISBN 0-8234-0287-8

The Beaver: How He Works

THE BEAVER is an animal well known for his industrious habits. A large beaver may weigh as much as fifty or sixty pounds, but most are somewhat smaller. At one time they were much sought after by fur trappers and Indians, who sold the pelts for a considerable profit.

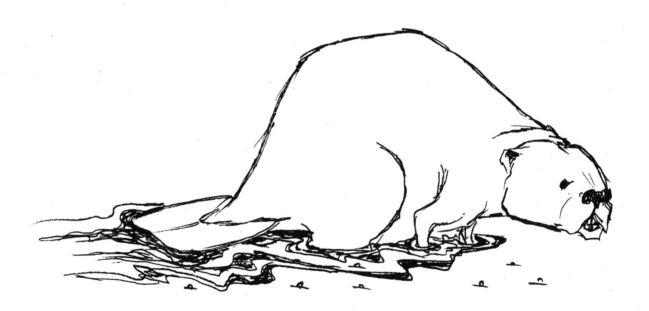

The beaver's large chisel-shaped front teeth and powerful neck muscles make him a very efficient woodcutter. Working on land, floating on the surface of a pond or even underwater, he fells trees and cuts them into sections as neatly as any woodsman.

One of the beaver's most noticeable characteristics is his broad flat scaly tail, which is very strong and very handy. He uses it as a sculling oar or as a rudder while swimming—and as a balancing pole while carrying loads of building material on land.

He also uses it as a prop when he cuts down a tree, or turns it under himself and sits on it. And in time of danger he can, by slapping a sharp blow to the surface of the water, give an alarm signal that can be heard for a surprisingly long distance. However, there is no truth in the old stories about his using his broad tail as a trowel when plastering his dam or his lodge.

The beaver, unlike most animals, makes no secret of the fact
when he becomes your new neighbor. Like an ambitious farmer, he starts
improving and rearranging his property almost at once. He cuts down
trees and bushes, leaving the stumps and piles of bright chips for all
to see.

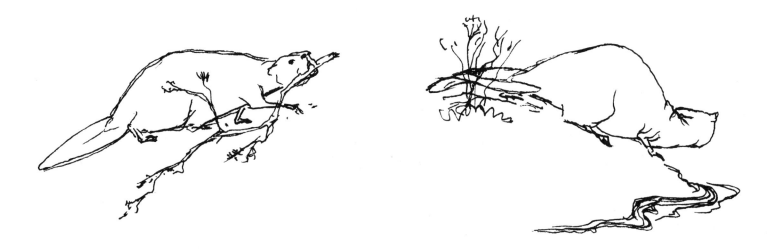

He builds dams to back up water for his own convenience, making
life difficult for users of dens, pathways, and gardens in the neighborhood.
He dredges canals and deepens waterways and changes the entire
appearance of the neighborhood.

As a new settler, however, one of the first things he does is dig a burrow in the stream bank for temporary living quarters. Starting near the bottom of the stream, he digs a tunnel slanting upwards, neatly gnawing through any roots that get in his way.

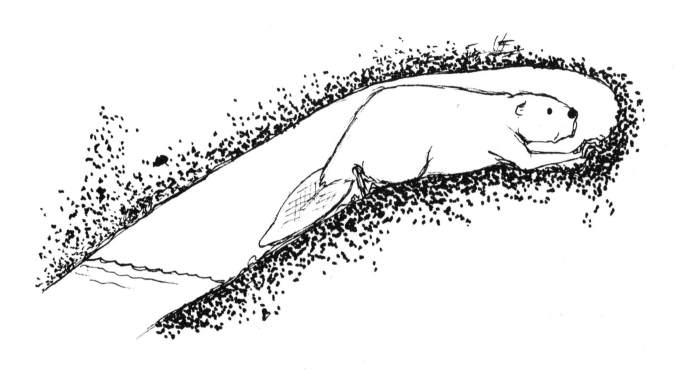

In the dry earth of the bank, well above the level of the stream, he hollows out a sleeping chamber the size of a bushel basket. The water-filled lower end of the entrance tunnel, or plunge hole, keeps out drafts and unwelcome visitors, while air for ventilation filters down through the earth around the tree roots overhead.

To go outside, he simply dives headfirst down through the plunge hole in his bedroom floor, swims a way along the stream bottom, and comes to the surface well out of reach of any danger on the bank.

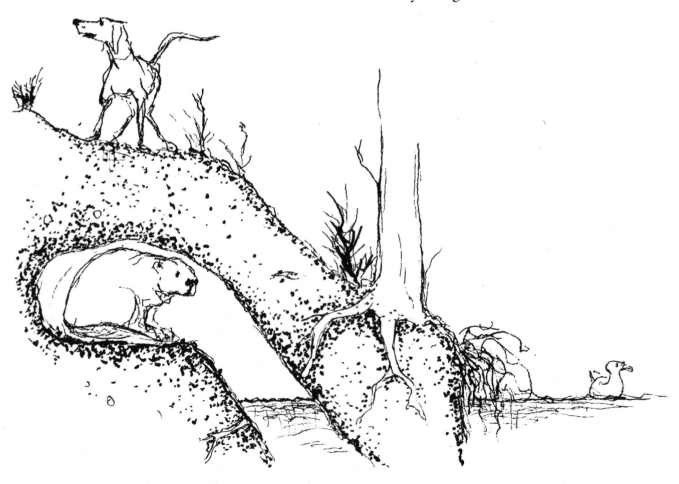

The finished burrow makes a safe and comfortable place for the beaver to sleep, or to loaf in time of danger or bad weather. Passersby seldom suspect that his living quarters may be just underfoot.

Being somewhat slow moving and clumsy on land, the beaver likes
to travel and work in or near deep water. Also, he finds it easier to float
branches and sticks to his work sites than to drag them over dry
ground. So, if the stream is small, he soon sets out to build a dam to
back up water for a pond.

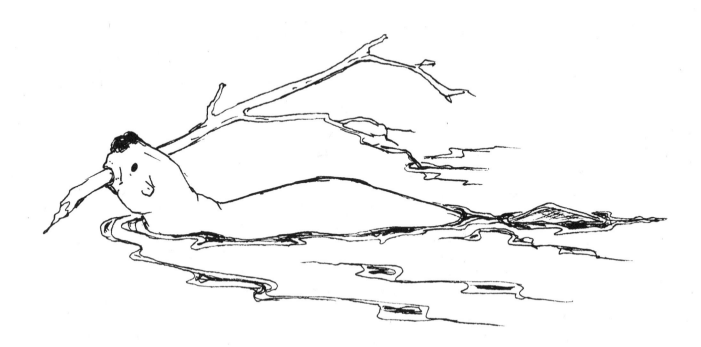

He is famous for his dam building, but his methods are somewhat
misunderstood. Instead of surveying a site as a man would, driving piling
and digging foundations, the beaver uses the simpler log-jam principle.
For building material he uses whatever is handy—tree branches,
sticks, brush, water plants, and mud.

Muttering and mumbling to himself, he splashes about in the water,
using his front paws and his teeth to push and tug sticks into place,
jamming them into the muddy banks, and weighting ends down with
mud and trash. If a piece is dislodged and carried away by the current,
the beaver makes no effort to bring it back. Easy come, easy go
seems to be his attitude.

While he doesn't give the appearance of really knowing what he
is about, the beaver soon manages to get a small tangle of sticks and
trash more or less firmly anchored across the stream. This coarse
construction interferes very little with the flow of the water,
but he seems not to mind.

From upstream he brings loads of finer material, leafy branches,
dead twigs, weed stems and other trash—anything that will catch in the
small log jam he has started.

Letting the force of the current help him, he pokes and shoves this
material under and between the pieces already in place, making a tightly
interlocked tangle, but one that still lets the water flow freely through it.

But now the beaver comes from a trip upstream with a muddy bundle
of rotting water plants, leaves, and streamers of briar clasped tightly
to his chest. Dropping the load in the water, he lets the force of
the current carry it against the face of the dam.

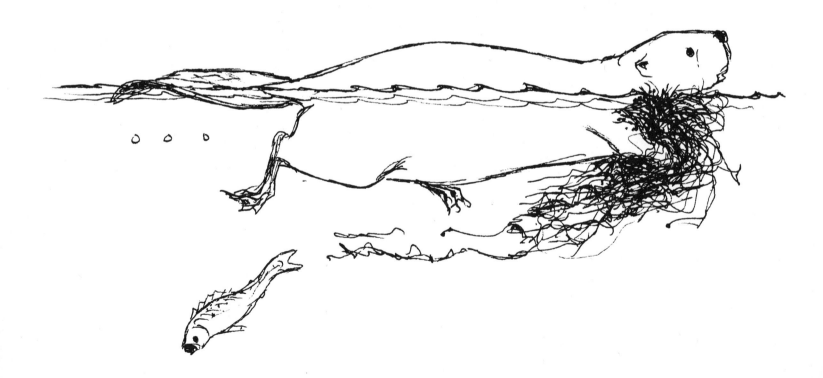

Some of the material passes through the structure and is carried downstream, but as the beaver brings additional loads, the strainer-like construction begins to clog, and before long a thick soggy mat covers the upstream side of the little dam. The flow of water is slowed somewhat, but much still leaks through.

As the flow of water through his dam is slowed, the beaver begins
hauling mud from the bottom of the pond and piling it onto the layer
of soggy trash. As the layer of mud thickens, it fills the hundreds of tiny
leaks and the water begins at last to back up behind the dam.

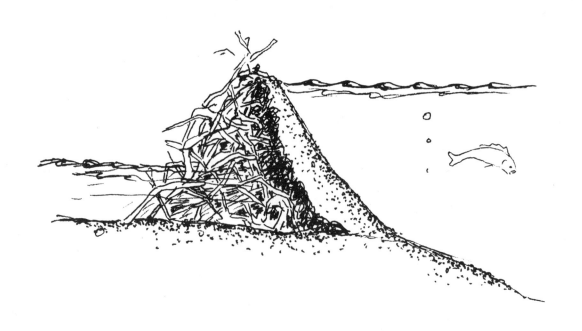

This first small dam has raised the water level only a few inches but the beaver, excavating for mud, has lowered the stream bottom also. So already he has a good beginning for the sort of pond he likes.

However, in spite of his reputation for busyness, the beaver is not by any means a steady worker, and even this small dam was not built all at once. He has a big appetite, and a great part of his time is spent in the search for food.

He is a vegetarian and likes variety in his diet. So in the course of a single meal, he moves from place to place along the stream. For an appetizer, he may search below the dam for the leaves and tender twigs of some particular bush that he fancies. Finished with that, he may move unhurriedly upstream and cut a green sapling of maple or bay from one of the thickets there.

He eats only the tender tips of the green twigs and the bark of the larger branches, leaving behind a litter of neatly peeled white sticks when he's finished. For still more variety, he dabbles about in the muddy shallows for the crisp roots and stems of different kinds of water plants.

He is also a great loafer, seeming always ready to stop work to watch
what his neighbors are doing. And, especially in early morning or evening,
he seems to thoroughly enjoy just doing nothing at all. But even so, in
his unhurried way, he does make great changes in his surroundings.

Each night, between interruptions for meals and other chores, the beaver inspects his new dam several times. Wherever he finds water running over the top, he piles on more sticks and mud until he temporarily stops the flow.

The stream itself helps him with his work by bringing him all manner of free building material. Tree trunks, dead branches, silt and other trash dislodged by rains or the rising level of the pond float downstream and are caught by the dam, ready for the beaver's use.

So, inch by inch, night by night, the dam continues to grow.

To strengthen his growing dam against the increasing weight of the
water behind it, the beaver braces the downstream side with longer sticks
he shoves over the top. The butts are jammed firmly into the stream
bottom and the tops, weighted down by mud, become a solid part
of the dam itself.

As the level of the pond rises, the backed-up water overflows the stream
banks and small trickles start escaping around the ends of the dam.
But when the beaver discovers this, he simply rakes up low dykes of
grass, weeds, and mud to stop the leaks. So, as the dam grows higher it
also grows longer.

As his pond grows, spreading out over the low ground on either side
of the stream, the beaver begins to feel more secure. And before long, in
addition to his other projects, he will start building a permanent lodge
to replace the temporary burrow dug in the bank.

And here again his building methods are entirely his own. Where
possible, he likes to build his lodge where it will be surrounded by water.
If there is no suitable island handy, he may build his own of mud
and sticks, in shallow water. Or, if he can find no better place, he may
build on the bank itself.

But, whatever the location, his method will be the same. Instead of putting up walls and a roof, he simply starts gathering together what appears to be nothing more than a trash pile on the spot where his lodge will be. Sticks, branches, and even parts of tree trunks are piled in a wild higgle piggle, crisscrossed and pointing in all directions.

As the ragged-looking pile grows, the beaver hauls mud dredged from the stream bottom and tramples it into the open spaces, between the tangled sticks and timbers.

As the beaver dredges mud from the bottom for his building operation, he also deepens and improves his pond. At the same time he undermines the roots of trees and bushes drowned by the rising water.

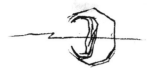

When these finally topple, he floats comfortably on the surface of the
water and gnaws the trunks and branches into manageable lengths.
Floating and dragging them to his building site, he adds them to the
growing pile that will be his lodge.

He seems to make slow progress because, as is his way, he divides his
time between this job, work on his dam, dredging new canals, searching
for food, and just plain loafing. But little by little, the ragged structure
grows until it is three or four feet high and ten or twelve feet across.

At this stage it is nothing more than a solid pile of sticks and mud so tightly packed as to be almost impossible to pull apart. And inside there is still no sign of any room or space for living quarters.

But now the beaver starts a tunnel from near the bottom of the stream, slanting upwards to the underside of the mound. He bores his way through the packed mud and sticks like some busy woodworking machine, making a neat round passageway only a little larger than his body.

Just above water level, he gnaws and digs out a good-sized vestibule. This will be a fine place to loaf or, in bad weather, to feed on the bark of branches and bushes brought in from outside. Upwards from this entrance hall, he bores another round passageway leading higher into the mound, where he hollows out an upstairs sleeping chamber.

When he is finished, the beaver has a safe weatherproof house too
strong to be broken into by any but the most determined enemy. The
only way in or out is through the water-filled plunge hole leading
to the deep water of the pond. In good weather, the top of the mound
is a pleasant place to take his meals or simply to watch the activities
of his neighbors.

And when winter comes, locking the pond under a thick cover of ice, the snow makes an insulating blanket that helps keep the inside of the lodge warm and comfortable. From outside, the only sign that the place is occupied comes from the slight melting around the tiny vents where the beaver's warm breath finds its way outside.

If he tires of being cooped up inside the lodge, the beaver can go down through his underwater passageway and swim under the ice to inspect his dam or visit one of his bank burrows with no one the wiser. If he feels hungry, he simply carries home a green branch from the supply he stored on the bottom of the pond earlier in the fall, and peels away the rich bark in the comfort of his vestibule.

With his dam in good condition, his lodge secure and surrounded on
all sides by deep water, the beaver has little to worry about. So during
the bitter weather he divides his time between eating and sleeping,
while he waits for spring and the beginning of another busy summer.

GLEN ROUNDS was born in the Badlands of South Dakota and spent his boyhood on a ranch in Montana. He then prowled around the country as a sign painter, cowpuncher, mule skinner, logger, carnival barker, and lightning artist. He has written many nature books for children, among them *Beaver Business*, *Wild Orphan*, *Lone Muskrat*, and *Wildlife at Your Doorstep*. He is also a master storyteller, well known as the author-illustrator of *Ol' Paul, the Mighty Logger*, *The Day the Circus Came to Lone Tree*, and *Mr. Yowder and the Lion Roar Capsules*.

He lives in Southern Pines, North Carolina, where he collects the material for his nature books.